Love Is...

To Bonnie,
   You are a beautiful
person. I enjoy you.
You have the gift
of wisdom. Keenan
is blessed with you.

        Love Always,
        Laurie L.

Love Is...

by
Laurie Lechlitner

Christian Publishing Services, Inc.
Tulsa, Oklahoma

Love Is...
ISBN 0-88144-125-2
Copyright © 1988 by Laurie Lechlitner
P. O. Box 852
Wakarusa, Indiana 46573

Published by Christian Publishing Services, Inc.
P.O. BOx 55388
Tulsa, Oklahoma 74155-1388

Dedication and Acknowledgment

I would like to dedicate this book, first of all, to my Lord. Without Him, I would not be an author.

I would also like to dedicate it to my dear husband, Brian, who has spent many late nights reading my material.

I would like to thank my beloved mentor, Terry Hatfield, who is also my spiritual father, for his advice and loving support.

And a special thanks goes to Ocella Pletcher, who believed in me enough to encourage me to write this book.

Contents

Contents

Foreword

The phone rang, and as I answered I heard the familiar voice of my friend, Ocella. She's a faithful friend. She and her husband, Luke, are the "salt of the earth." She was so excited.

"Laurie, I read your poem, 'Love Is...' she said. "I prayed about it, and I feel the Lord wants you to write a book by the same title. You could have twelve chapters and title them by the first lines of the stanzas in your poem."

Ocella walks and talks with the Lord. I knew that the words from her mouth were sent by a Higher Source.

So, here I am writing a book. Writing is a hobby of mine. I started out writing little articles for my adult Sunday school class. The people from the Messenger Class are some of my dearest friends, and when I discovered that they enjoyed my articles, I kept them supplied with a steady flow of them.

For seven years, my husband, Brian, and I have been involved in (what we call) the institution ministry. We visit prisons and hospitals for the mentally and physically handicapped. This is my second year as a licensed minister in the Church of the Brethren. I heard the Lord calling me to become a shepherd of His flock.

When it comes to learning, I am a sponge. I read and listen — and the material "sticks." I love the Word of God and can spend hours at a time studying it. My writing is one of the outlets for the information I gain from my study, as well as for my own feelings. I am a person who needs a means of self-expression. I also preach a sermon once a week at a health-care center and teach a Bible study and Sunday school class at my home church, Baugo Church, in Wakarusa, Indiana.

I've learned many things in the course of my faith pilgrimage. But the thing I consider to be most important is expressed by the Apostle Paul in Philippians 4:13: **I can do everything through him who gives me strength.**

The purpose of this book is to share God's love — and mine — with you.

Love in Christ,
Laurie Lechlitner

Love Is...

Love is a jagged thorn that pierces the heart. It causes pain when it enters deep. Love is the pounding of nails in outstretched hands and feet. It is the thrust of a sword in our sides.

To love is to become vulnerable. It is to give another human being your heart to keep and possibly break.

Real love is unconditional. It matters not whether the love is returned. Real love grows stronger when it is tried and rejected. The roots go deeper.

Love is a passionate fire. It gives us x-ray eyes to see a person's full potential and to never be satisfied till they reach it.

Love is a rock. It is not moved during the storms and strong winds.

Love is commitment. It is the willingness to walk through life with another.

Love is a union of spirits. We can feel another's pain. Love gives divine discernment to bear another's burden and the joy to carry it long distances.

Love is tough enough to bring out the best in another without worrying about being popular in their eyes or even whether they respect our opinion at the time.

Love is a motivator. People are like roses, when they are cherished and cared for, they blossom in beauty.

Love is a mother giving birth. It is painful, but new life emerges.

Love is the powerful force that created the universe and then became a part of that creation to die for mankind.

Yes, love is God. In order to know Him we will experience the thorn of love in our hearts, but we will know the deep joy of new life.

Laurie Lechlitner

Dear friends, let us love one another, for love is from God. Everyone who loves has been born of God and knows God. Whoever does not love does not know God, for God is love.

1 John 4:7,8

Love is patient, love is kind. It does not envy, it does not boast, it is not proud. It is not rude, it is not self-seeking, it is not easily angered, it keeps no record of wrongs. Love does not delight in evil but rejoices with the truth. It always protects, always trusts, always hopes, always perseveres.

Love never fails....

1 Corinthians 13:4-8

...perfect love drives out fear....

1 John 4:18

We love because he first loved us.

1 John 4:19

"Greater love has no one than this, that one lay down his life for his friends."

John 15:13

"All men will know that you are my disciples if you love one another."

John 13:35

1

Love Is a Jagged Thorn

"Love is the most terrible, and also the most generous of the passions; it is the only one that includes in its dreams the happiness of someone else."

J.A. Karr

Jesus is the Good Shepherd. He lays down His life for His sheep.

This is my second year as a licensed minister. I am working hard towards ordination. When I first entered the ministry, I remember praying, "Lord, give me a shepherd's heart." At the time, I really didn't know what I was asking. I saw other ministers who had such compassion for the flock. I wanted to love as they did. But I didn't realize the pain I would experience as a result of that love.

Love, in its deepest form, is like a jagged thorn that pierces your heart. It hurts as it penetrates your inmost being. It feels like a knife that cuts you all the way to your spirit, to the secret place where your deepest emotions and motives are hidden. It exposes you for all the world to see.

Some never take the chance of loving this deeply. They are not willing to devote their lives to another person because they are not willing to bear the pain. The pain of deep love would be unbearable if it were not mixed with joy and sweetness. There is a satisfaction in loving deeply that no one can know without experiencing the pain that goes with that love.

This deep love is something that is given to us from above. It is not something we ourselves can produce, or even control. It is the love Jesus displayed when He was hanging on the cross. He was in so much pain and agony. He was crushed all the way to His spirit. But in the very midst of His pain and suffering He uttered those words of selfless love: "Father, forgive them; they don't know what they are doing." That stabbing love gave Jesus compassion for the very human race which was at that moment driving spikes into His hands and feet.

Yes, love is like a jagged thorn. It hurts and throbs. It is so deep that it is often misunderstood and even ridiculed. It seeks the best for another without trying to control him. This deepest form of love gives us marathon endurance. When a stab of pain shoots through our being, we get a "second wind," like an athlete who is in training to run a great distance. When we catch our second wind, the joy is unbelievably sweet. It makes the sweat and effort and pain all worthwhile.

When God chose Mary to be the mother of our Lord, He bestowed upon her this highest form of love. He knew that, as the mother of the Messiah, she would need it. Jesus suffered more than anyone on earth has ever suffered, but I believe dear Mary suffered almost as severely as her Son.

Mary loved deeply. I know she walked very close to God because that is where this great capacity to love comes from. When the angel told Mary that she would be the mother of the Savior, she must have felt the thorn of pain, but the joy of devotion.

Mary was in love with a carpenter from Nazareth to whom she was engaged to be married. How do you explain to your fiance that you are expecting a child that isn't his? How do you convince him that this child is conceived of the Holy Spirit?

The love Mary felt for Joseph cut her heart like a knife when he threatened to break off the engagement. But the wonderful part of this deep love from God is that it binds broken relationships and draws like a magnet. Joseph received a divine revelation of Christ through Mary's love. So he took Mary to be his wife.

When we love totally and completely, people will always see Christ in us.

After Jesus was born, Joseph and Mary took Him to the temple in Jerusalem to dedicate Him to God. Can you imagine their feelings as they carried this beautiful baby up to the temple? They must have felt so proud, yet overwhelmed. How do you go about raising the Son of God?

As they entered the temple, they were met by Simeon. He too possessed this great and painful love in his heart. It was this love which made him a prophet, a seer. Love gives us eyes that see things others miss. At the temple, there were children coming and going all the time. But Simeon instantly recognized his Lord. When he saw the holy child, his heart throbbed with overwhelming devotion.

Simeon is very truthful with Mary as he gazes upon her baby. His words to her are recorded in Luke 2:34-35:

> . . ."This child is destined to cause the falling and rising of many in Israel, and to be a sign that will be spoken against, so that the thoughts of many hearts will be revealed. And a sword will pierce your own soul too."

Oh, how familiar that feeling is to me — when a sword pierces the heart. Simeon was absolutely right. He knew the deep love that hurts. Mary also understood that pain.

Mary walked through life with a painful thorn in her heart, pierced through by a sword that caused her heart to bleed. When Jesus started His public ministry, she found that she could not stand in His way. When she saw that she was not able to position herself between Him and the crowds to keep Him from being opposed and persecuted, she learned that real love does not try to control the object of its love. She felt the deep hurt of ridicule when He was laughed at. She felt the agony of rejection when her own friends and neighbors tried to throw her Son off a cliff. She felt severe dread and anxiety when the Pharisees tried to kill Him. She knew His sorrow at the hard-heartedness of His own people who refused to turn to Him to be saved. Deep love is able to empathize with the loved one, to feel his deepest feelings.

Mary's darkest day was the one she spent at the foot of the cross. When the spikes were driven into the hands and feet of her Son, it was Mary's heart which was being nailed to the cross of Calvary. She sobbed as He suffered and bled, because her heart was also suffering and bleeding. When He cried out for water, her own soul was athirst. Her agony was so great that when He said, "It is finished," she must have sunk to the ground, drained of all her strength.

The pain was great for Mary, but there is strength in deep love. There is also divine hope. Because she loved deeply, Mary was able to see the glorious resurrection of her beloved Son. The thorn of pain became a seed of joy that produced a hundredfold return.

In order to know the great joy of love, we must suffer the great pain of love. We must endure the agony of the cross before we can experience the ecstasy of the resurrection.

2
Love Is Vulnerable

"Love makes obedience lighter than liberty."

R.W. Alger

First Corinthians 13 is the "love chapter" of the Bible. There are many characteristics of love. One of them is trust. A great deal of trust goes into love relationships.

When we love someone, we give our heart to that person. In so doing, we give him or her the power to break our heart.

An insecure person has a hard time with this particular concept of love. He builds protective walls around himself to guard against hurt. But these walls also keep out true love and enthusiasm.

To give another person our heart is to let that person see deep inside of us. He or she sees our strengths, but also gets a full view of our weaknesses. By opening ourselves to love, we risk ridicule and misunderstanding. But when someone truly loves us in return, we have the satisfaction of experiencing unconditional love. We know that we are loved as we are — "warts and all."

Some try to keep others at arm's length, never letting them get close. Such people fear rejection. But one thing the Lord has shown me in my spiritual walk is that, although rejection is painful, it is not fatal. Rejection is not the end of the world.

I love the old saying, "It is better to have loved and lost than never to have loved at all." There is so much truth in that statement. Even if our love is not returned, we are richer for having given ourselves. There is no gift more satisfying than sacrificial love.

C.S. Lewis gives us a marvelous description of love:

"To love at all is to be vulnerable. Love anything, and your heart will certainly be wrung and possibly broken. If you want to make sure of keeping it intact, you must give your heart to no one, not even an animal. Wrap it carefully round with hobbies and little luxuries; avoid all entanglements; lock it safe in the casket or coffin of selfishness. But in that casket — safe, dark, motionless, airless — it will change. It will not be broken; it will become unbreakable, impenetrable, irredeemable — The only place outside Heaven where you can be perfectly safe from all the dangers of love is Hell."

Without love, life is a living hell. Never to give of ourselves makes us shallow, fearful and selfish people. We are miserable and have missed the whole purpose of our existence.

Jesus knew human beings better than any of us ever will. Why? Because He is the Creator of all life. He is God. But He showed us how to live. His heart was broken and shattered by mankind. He didn't die because of His crucifixion. He died of a broken heart. Pilate was shocked to hear that Jesus had died so quickly on the cross. The soldiers had to break the legs of the other two victims before they would succumb to death. But with Jesus that was not necessary. That's because He died in perfect love; He was the most vulnerable person who ever lived. He was also the most hurting.

But along with the agony there is the ecstasy. The Bible tells us that it was for the joy that was before Him that He endured the cross. (Heb. 12:2.)

Jesus knew greater joy than any person in history. His greatest command was that we love one another:

"My command is this: Love each other as I have loved you. Greater love has no one than this, that one lay down his life for his friends."

John 15:12,13

The twelve disciples broke Jesus' heart many times. As a matter of fact, Judas was a complete failure, but Jesus loved him to the end. We will also meet our share of Judas Iscariots who will betray us with a kiss. We will also meet the Simon Peters who will deny ever knowing us. And there will be those trusted friends who will run away from us when they see that we are headed for the cross. But, even knowing that, we have nothing to fear in loving one another. Why? Because perfect love casts out fear. (1 John 4:18.) Because, as disciples of Christ, our ultimate goal is not self-protection but the bringing out of the best in the ones we love. Of working for their good by putting their welfare before our own — by choice.

The Apostle Peter denied Jesus three times, but because God's love never gives up, Peter was transformed. He laid down his life for the sake of the Gospel and, according to tradition, was crucified upside down because he considered himself unworthy of being crucified in the same manner as his Lord.

Can you imagine the joyful reunion with his beloved Savior that awaited Peter as he entered the gates of heaven? Yes, love is worth the pain of being vulnerable. Because of our love for others, we will welcome many a brother and sister into the Kingdom of God.

When we love, we give our heart to the one loved. We make ourselves vulnerable because we give that person permission to do with our heart as he or she will. Sometimes our heart is broken. But there is joy even in the pain of love.

I would like to close this chapter with a quote from H. W. Beecher:

"We never know how much one loves until we know how much he is willing to endure and suffer for us; and it is the suffering element that measures love. The characters that are great, must of necessity, be characters that shall be willing, patient, and strong to endure for others — To hold our nature in the willing service of another, is the divine idea of manhood, of the human character."

3
Love Is Unconditional

"True love is eternal, infinite, and always like itself. It is equal and pure, without violent demonstrations: it is seen with white hair and is always young in the heart."

Honore de Balzac

Some see God as a fierce ogre standing with a club in His hand ready to "clobber" anyone who gets "out of line." It hurts me when I meet people who have this false conception. In talking with them, I have found that they have one thing in common: they seem to have come from a very unloving, judgmental family environment. Often I find that there was a lack of communication in their families. As they were growing up, they did not experience a loving relationship with their own fathers.

I used to work at a day-care center, and I noticed a sharp difference between those children with loving fathers and those who had unloving fathers, or no father image at all. I firmly believe that our relationship with our heavenly Father is greatly affected by the relationship we have with our earthly fathers. I find that children who do not feel loved by their earthly fathers usually react to the Gospel in one of two ways: Either they wrestle for the love of God, as Jacob did because his father favored his brother, or they blossom because of their realization that God loves them unconditionally.

On the wall of my living room there hangs a framed picture of Jesus which was drawn for me by an adolescent inmate of a state hospital for the mentally disturbed. In the portrait, the eyes are cruel and piercing and the features are large and exaggerated. The young man who drew it is very maladjusted. He has never known the love of an earthly father. I am working wth him to change that image of God in his mind from one of a fierce, mean tyrant to one of a gentle Shepherd Who loves him dearly.

I can't help but think that God sent His Son into a loving household. Although we hear very little about Joseph and suppose that he died while Jesus was still growing up, I know in my heart that he was a loving earthly father to our Lord. We never hear of his being harsh with his foster Son, even when twelve-year-old Jesus was found in the temple after being separated from his parents for three whole days. (Luke 2:41-50.)

I am so excited to know that my Lord loves me unconditionally. He loves me "warts and all." I am a perfectionist and tend to be very hard on myself at times. I strive for excellence in everything I do and sometimes I become quite discouraged when I feel that I don't measure up to my own high standards. But I have found that my heavenly Father is not nearly as demanding as I am. After a discouraging day, I will sit in the presence of the Lord and realize that He is proud of me just the way I am. He is never as hard on me as I am on myself. When I realize His strong love for me, I can handle anything that comes my way. He not only loves me, He also *likes* me.

Jesus is the Master of love. He loves uncondi- tionally. There are many examples of His great love for

His group of twelve disciples. They were a bickering bunch. They argued about who was the greatest among them and even questioned Jesus' messages. Peter was interested in receiving a reward for his services. In Matthew 19:27 we read that he asked Jesus what he was going to get for following Him. These twelve men were under a great deal of stress and often grew tired of the crowds. They wanted to call down fire and brimstone upon those who opposed their Master, and even tried to drive away the children who wanted to come to Jesus. But the heavenly Father called Jesus to work this disagreeable group into a harmonious unit. It is amazing the love Jesus showed for those men. If anything in the world will transform a person, it is the unconditional love of Jesus.

Two of the toughest cases were Peter and Judas. Peter was so impulsive. He did a lot of boasting, but when he was put to the test, he failed every time. He seemed to have great faith, even enough to walk on water, but in the face of the wind and storms of life, he sank like a rock. Peter loved Jesus, but not quite as much as he loved Peter.

At the Last Supper, we see Peter telling Jesus, "I will die for You." But a few hours later, in order to save his own skin, Peter denies that he even knows the Lord. Not once, but three times. Yet Jesus tells him, "You are Peter (a rock), and on this rock I will build My Church. Feed My sheep and care for your brothers."

Many of us would disown a person who would deny us in our hour of greatest need. But this unconditional love transformed Peter from a cowardly boaster who denied his Lord into a humble martyr who gave his life for the sake of the Gospel.

It is hard enough to love Peter, but imagine loving Judas Iscariot. Jesus knew mankind so well. He knew about Judas from the beginning. In John 6:70,71 Jesus says to His disciples: ...**"Have I not chosen you, the Twelve? Yet one of you is a devil!" (He meant Judas, the son of Simon Iscariot, who, though one of the Twelve, was later to betray him).**

Although Jesus knew about Judas, He loved him as much as He loved the others. He never embarrassed Judas by singling him out and revealing his true nature to the other eleven. As a matter of fact, Jesus honored Judas more than He did the rest. Judas was chosen to be the trusted treasurer of the group. John tells us in his Gospel that Judas would steal from the treasury and use the money for his own greedy purposes. (John 12:6.) Even when Judas betrayed Him, Jesus loved him. There was hurt in His eyes and on His face as He said, "Judas, must you betray Me with a kiss?"

God's love takes more time with the lost. Jesus told the Pharisees that He came to save the lost, not the self-righteous. He is the Shepherd Who leaves the ninety-nine who are safely in the fold to go out and search for the one that is lost. When that one is found, there is more rejoicing in heaven over his salvation than over the ninety-nine who did not go astray. (Luke 15:7.)

In Matthew 13:24-30, Jesus presents the parable of the weeds. In verse 36-43 He explains its meaning to His disciples: The good seed are those people planted by the Father. The weeds are the wicked ones planted by the devil. The field is the world. In this life, the good and the evil are mixed together. The Father loves sinners too much to root them up. He gives them a lifetime to come to Him to receive His transforming love.

Sometimes when I really "blow it," I'm so happy for God's great love. I can "pull the wool" over the eyes of my brothers and sisters, but God sees the real me. He sees my inner thoughts and motives. He knows me, just as Jesus knew Judas. But I love the way He deals with me. In my spirit, I feel Him say: "I love you so much, Laurie. We need to smooth out those rough places in your life. If you will put yourself in My hands, I'll work with you and mold you to perfection."

I wonder how anyone can turn down the offer of such a great love. Jesus holds out His nail-scarred hands and says to each of us: "I want to love you just the way you are. I stand at your heart's door and knock. When you invite Me in, to be your Savior and Lord of your life, you will know My love that fills the void in your heart."

I am so glad I invited Jesus into my heart. At age 12 I received His love. I simply said: "Jesus, I want to live for You. Come into my heart and love me." And He did! He has been loving me ever since. His love is real, and it's unconditional. Praise the Lord!

4

Love Is a Passionate Fire

"Love was to his impassioned soul, not a mere part of its existence, but the whole, the very life-breath of his heart."

Moore

". . . He will baptize you with the Holy Spirit and with fire."

Luke 3:16

Love is not passive. It is an active force. When you love someone, you expect the best from him. Love does not sit quietly by and allow the loved one to die in his sins. Love creates an active passion and zeal to see the objects of its love mature in faith, to become all the Father created them to be.

I have watched many movies and passion plays about the life of Jesus. I am disappointed that the Son of God is so often portrayed as a man sitting serenely, surrounded by admiring followers. I think this is a distorted view of our Lord. Such depictions provide only a dim, one-sided view of Jesus. Most of His life was spent in conflict. We learn so much as we watch the Master deal with the battles of love.

Luke 3:16 tells us that Jesus will baptize us with the Holy Spirit and with fire. The purpose of the fire is to burn up the chaff. True love is a refining fire that consumes the dross and brings us forth as gold. That is why many resisted Jesus. The fire is uncomfortable, sometimes downright painful. But, oh, how necessary!

Jesus was so full of fiery passion. His zeal was for mankind to get a total view of the Father. Isn't it ironic that when God came to earth in human flesh, He wasn't recognized by the very ones who studied the scriptures so diligently?

Some of us will avoid conflict at all costs. If we were to see the proud Pharisees coming toward us, I am afraid that most of us would begin to look for a place to run and hide. Not Jesus. He cared too much to avoid conflict. He met His adversaries face to face and even called them blind guides and whitewashed tombs. Love sees what a person can become, but it never overlooks obvious or hidden sin.

I think if I could choose to observe any situation in the life of Jesus, I would like to see Him as He overturned the tables of the money changers in the temple. In reading this account in Matthew 21:12-14, we can learn some valuable lessons about conflict management, and also see the passionate fire of true love:

> **Jesus entered the temple area and drove out all who were buying and selling there. He overturned the tables of the money changers and the benches of those selling doves. "It is written," he said to them, " 'My house will be called a house of prayer,' but you are making it a 'den of robbers.' "**
>
> **The blind and lame came to him at the temple, and he healed them.**

Since it was Jesus Who gave us many of our basic principles of peace, it sometimes seems hard to fathom how He could knock over tables and chairs and chase people out of the temple. But I believe He was showing us that many times without head-on confrontation there can be no lasting peace. How many of us suffer today from physical and emotional disorders which are a direct result of squelching our inner feelings?

Jesus loved the people too much to allow them to desecrate God's house. But He didn't just knock over tables and drive out the merchants without explaining His position or motivation. He backed up His actions with references from the Word of God. He quoted scriptures from Isaiah and Jeremiah to make it clear to the people that they were misusing the house of God. The temple was not a market. It was meant for prayer.

In my mind's eye I can see the anger and hurt that must have been written across the face of our Lord as He explained the proper use of the house of God. But I also see the look of love in His eyes. Even in His disciplining, there is such an awareness of His love.

It is beautiful how Jesus resolved this conflict. He called the people in for healing. After every fiery conflict, there is a need for the gentle touch of a healing hand.

After this episode in the temple, the Jewish leaders began to make plans to kill Jesus. There have always been those who have sought to extinguish the fiery passion of love. But even after the crucifixion, it lives on! No human being can put out the fire of love. All the powers of hell will not stop its passion and zeal.

Love is a passionate fire. It is never satisfied until its beloved is walking in the image of God.

5

Love Is a Rock

"Two sentiments alone suffice for man, were he to live the age of the rocks — love, and the contemplation of the deity."

Watts

Christians are a strong breed of people. They stand when others fall. They persevere when others give up.

In Matthew 16:18 Jesus tells us, **". . .on this rock I will build my church, and the gates of Hades** (the powers of hell) **will not overcome it."** That "rock" on which the Church is founded is love. Love is sturdy and dependable. It will not give way under us. It is hard to walk in shifting sand, but solid rock is a support under our feet.

One reason Jesus came to earth was to correct man's concept of the Father and of salvation. The Jews worshipped God and had His written laws. Moses tells us that whoever lives by these laws is in fellowship with God. Christ came to fulfill the Law. He doesn't tell us to "chuck" the Ten Commandments, but He tells us their real purpose — to turn people to Him, the Savior.

When a Jewish religious leader asked Jesus, **"Teacher, which is the greatest commandment in the Law?"** (Matt. 22:36), **Jesus replied: " 'Love the Lord your God with all your heart and with all your soul and with all your mind.' This is the first and greatest commandment. And the second is like it: 'Love your**

neighbor as yourself.' All the Law and the Prophets hang on these two commandments" (vv. 37-40).

Here Jesus was showing the people of His day God's intention in giving the Ten Commandments. He was exchanging the external code, written on tablets of stone, for an internal spirit, written on hearts of flesh. What a revelation!

We love God because He first loved us. (1 John 4:19.) This is the rock upon which our faith is built. We have a foundation when we accept the love of God through His Son, Jesus Christ, Who has told us:

> **"Whoever has my commands and obeys them, he is the one who loves me...."**
>
> **John 14:21**

Jesus makes it very clear that we are to obey His commands. He teaches love and peace. As the Apostle John has noted, we cannot say we love God Whom we cannot see if we hate our brothers whom we can see. (1 John 4:20.)

Our Christian foundation is love. This is the rock upon which our lives are built so that we do not fall when the storms of life hit us.

Love causes us to be able to stand up under great opposition. We have a message to share with the world that is more important than life and limb.

The Apostle Paul was firmly founded on the rock of love. The storm winds and flood waters never overcame him.

My favorite account of the strength of Paul is found in Acts 14:8-20. Here we find Paul and Barnabas in Lystra. It is Paul's first missionary journey, a great opportunity to share the message of the love of Jesus.

As Paul is speaking to the crowd, he sees a man crippled in his feet from birth. Paul reaches out with the healing hand of the love of Jesus, and the man is miraculously healed. When the crowd of Greeks see what Paul has done, they think he is a god. They bring a wreath to place on his head. They begin to get ready to make sacrifice to him, thinking he is the Greek god, Hermes.

With great difficulty, Paul stops the people from sacrificing to him; instead he tells them about Jesus and His love. But some Jewish legalists are present. The preaching of salvation by grace always angers a legalist, who sees salvation as being attained only by self-effort and personal "holiness." When Paul preaches Jesus Christ, he is upsetting the whole religious system of these devout Jews.

Many times, when we go to people in our own name, we are accepted and even honored. That is the worldly way. But often when we demonstrate the purifying love of Jesus Christ, the world is offended. This is exactly what happens to Paul here in Lystra. The carnal world, with its emphasis on religious rules and regulations, rejects the love of Christ and turns against the one who demonstrates it.

The pious Jews stone Paul and drag him out of the city, thinking he is dead. But anyone who knows Paul can tell you that he is not "whipped." He not only gets back up, he walks straight back into the city.

The love of Jesus was Paul's firm foundation. The storm winds and raging floods did not overwhelm him because he was founded on a rock.

A few chapters farther on, in the *King James Version* of Acts 17:6, we find the Jews in Thessalonica saying this about Paul and his companions: **...These that have turned the world upside down are come hither also.** Yes, the love of Jesus does indeed "turn the world upside down!"

In Matthew 7:24-27 Jesus says:

> **"Therefore everyone who hears these words of mine and puts them into practice is like a wise man who built his house on the rock. The rain came down, the streams rose, and the winds blew and beat against that house; yet it did not fall, because it had its foundation on the rock.**
>
> **"But everyone who hears these words of mine and does not put them into practice is like a foolish man who built his house on sand. The rain came down, the streams rose, and the winds blew against that house, and it fell with a great crash."**

The love of Jesus is a firm foundation. It is our rock.

6
Love Is Commitment

*"Love is the purification of the heart from self;
it strengthens and ennobles the character; gives
higher motive and nobler aim to every action of life,
and makes both man and woman strong, noble and
courageous. The power to love truly and devotedly
is the noblest gift with which a human being can
be endowed; but it is a sacred fire that must not
be burned to idols."*

Maria Jane Jewsbury

There are so many divorces and broken homes
these days. It is rare for me to talk to a child whose
parents are not divorced or getting a divorce. Many
"couples" live together, but are afraid of marriage.
Commitment is a word that is seldom used any more.
But commitment is the core of a love relationship. It
is the most important element. There is great joy in
commitment.

Jesus Christ is the beginning of real love. Without
Him, we sell our lives short. With Him, we learn what
life and love are really all about.

If there is one thing Jesus stressed throughout
His earthly ministry, it was a call to commitment.
Multitudes of people would come from miles away for
Jesus to feed them miraculously, heal them of their
diseases, cast demons out of them, and cure their

mental illnesses. But as soon as He began to talk about commitment, the ranks quickly thinned.

In the sixth chapter of John we read how Jesus miraculously fed 5,000 people with five loaves and two fish. The people went wild. They spread the report of the grand banquet to every itinerant in the area. Jesus soon became a real hero. All the freeloaders for miles around rushed after Him, followed closely by hoards of curiosity seekers. Also in the throngs were the religious leaders who came to spy on Him to make sure He was "playing by all the rules." So it was to a mixed crowd that Jesus uttered these memorable words: **"I am the bread of life....Whoever eats my flesh and drinks my blood....will live forever"** (John 6:35,54,58).

These people were Jews. They weren't ignorant pagans. They knew what He was talking about. They understood perfectly well that He was calling them to commitment. They knew He was speaking of a covenant relationship.

But what exactly is a *covenant*? In Jewish tradition, a covenant is an agreement sealed in blood. For example, when a covenant was made between two families, they were considered blood relatives who had joined their strengths together forever.

Marriage is a covenant relationship. In the marriage ceremony, a husband and wife are sealed together. Their union is blessed of God. Their children are a combination of both their blood lines.

A covenant is always based on love. Covenant love is very deep. It signifies a loyalty that says, "I will lay down my life for you." We should never enter a covenant lightly. It is binding. It is an agreement before

God that holds us accountable to Him and to our covenant partner.

The Bible is a book based on a covenant relationship between God and man. This covenant is sealed by the blood of Jesus. Thus, a covenant is a call to commitment.

In His words in John 6:35-58, Jesus was calling these people into a union, a covenant relationship, with Him. He would lay down His life for them, and they were to live for Him and carry His testimony to the whole world, even if it meant martyrdom.

From this time many of his disciples turned back and no longer followed him.

John 6:66

As we see in this verse, when commitment was mentioned, everybody retreated except a chosen few.

Many of us profess our love for Christ, but are we totally dedicated and committed to His cause? In many parts of the world, our commitment to Christ would be quickly put to the test. I wonder how committed we would remain with the barrel of a gun in our face? None of us like to think about that. But it is an essential point to ponder.

Jesus is calling us to total, not partial, commitment. We initiate that commitment simply by inviting Jesus into our hearts as our Savior and Lord. We continue that commitment by walking in obedience to Him.

It takes deep love for one person to commit himself totally to another. To stand beside the other person in the good and the bad. The joy and the sorrow. In health and in sickness. A marriage is that kind of a relationship. But there are also friendships which can be covenants, or agreements to love.

I love the story of Ruth. It is one of the most beautiful stories of committed love I have ever read. It portrays the wonderful friendship that existed between a young girl, Ruth, and her mother-in-law, Naomi.

Naomi was a survivor. She was a strong, independent woman who believed she could make it on her own. She didn't reach out to anybody for help. She had her husband and her two sons to provide for her, so she felt she "had the world by the tail." She could face anything life had to offer.

It is good that Naomi was so strong and adaptable, because there came a famine in the land of Judah where she lived so she and her family had to pack their belongings and move to Moab. Moabites were not very fond of Jews, and the Jews considered Moabites detestable. To Jews, Moabites were "pagan Gentiles," "unclean foreigners" who worshipped idols and ate forbidden foods.

I imagine it came as quite a shock to Naomi, once her family was settled in their new home, to learn that her two boys had their eyes on a pair of neighborhood Moabite girls. It was strictly against Jewish law to intermarry with "pagans." But Naomi loved her sons. They were her whole life, especially since her husband had died soon after their arrival in Moab. So marriages for the sons were arranged.

Soon after the marriages, Naomi's whole world fell apart. Within a short time, she lost both of her beloved sons to death. All she had left were her two daughters-in-law, Orpah and Ruth. She was in a stange land living among a strange people. She had no family ties in Moab at all.

When Naomi discovered that the famine was over in Judah, she became homesick for her own country. She decided to return to Judah. But she knew how her people felt about Moabites. It would never do to take her two sweet daughters-in-law back to Bethlehem with her. The people might harm them physically; they would certainly hurt them verbally. So Naomi kissed the girls goodbye and sent them back to their own people. Although it was a dangerous trip to make alone, she began to make preparations to set out on her long journey home.

Orpah dutifully obeys her mother-in-law and returns to her family. But not faithful Ruth. Instead, she utters one of the most beautful promises of commitment ever recorded. In Ruth 1:16,17 of the *King James Version* she says to Naomi:

> ...Intreat me not to leave thee, or to return from following after thee: for whither thou goest, I will go; and where thou lodgest, I will lodge: thy people shall be my people, and thy God my God.
>
> Where thou diest, will I die, and there will I be buried: the Lord do so to me, and more also, if ought but death part thee and me.

What a speech! That's commitment! That's love! Ruth knew what a risk she was taking. But, you see, God honors that kind of commitment. Ruth ended up marrying one of her late husband's relatives, a wealthy man of good standing in Bethlehem. Ruth is one of the few women mentioned by name in the direct genealogy of Jesus. (Matt. 1:5.)

Commitment is a decision to live one's life to make a difference in someone else's life. It is what Christian love is all about. It is choosing to love for a lifetime, and not just for the moment or as long as it is convenient or "fulfilling." Commitment is choosing to work through differences and not to give up and "bail out."

Commitment is the root of all lasting love.

7

Love Is a Union of Spirits

"With thee all toils are sweet; each clime hath charms; earth-sea alike — our world within our arms!"

Lord Byron

Did you ever meet a person for the first time with whom you were able to communicate perfectly? It seemed as if you had known each other for years. There was an instant bond of mutual affection and understanding.

This kind of person is what I call a kindred spirit. Kindred spirits flow in the same direction. There is love between them that is divine and God-given.

When we accept Jesus Christ into our hearts, we receive the Holy Spirit. We are united to all other Christians by the Spirit of Christ. But not all of our brothers and sisters in the Lord are kindred spirits. We are not always able to understand one another. This situation is not necessarily bad. It simply means that we see things from a different perspective.

I am reminded of an illustration I heard a while back. It describes this concept so well:

"If we live in the valley on one side of a mountain and our brother lives in the valley on the other side of the mountain, the scenery will be quite different, though we are looking at the same mountain."

45

I don't believe the Lord ever intended for us always to agree. Diversity is what makes the world interesting. A flower garden is never more beautiful than when it contains a variety of different-colored flowers.

I would like for us to look deeper into this beautiful union of kindred spirits. I have a dear friend into whose eyes I can look and tell exactly what he is thinking. We laugh at the same things and are able to "read between the lines" when we converse. When we are together, we can feel one another's emotions. I learned very early in our relationship not to wear a mask when I'm with my kindred spirit. He can see all the way to my inmost heart and can detect my most secret motives and desires. But, I can also see inside of him. This "gift of mutual discernment" is a sign of a very special love. With this union of spirits we can be ourselves; actually, we have no choice.

In his writings, the Apostle John often referred to himself as "the disciple whom Jesus loved." Jesus seemed to be able to communicate with John in a special way. For example, it was John who leaned back against the Lord's breast at the Last Supper to inquire who was going to betray Him. (John 13:21-25.) At the crucifixion, it was to John that Jesus entrusted His mother by simply saying, "Here is your mother." (John 19:27.) John knew what Jesus meant. He had a deep understanding of the Lord. That same verse tells us that from that day forth, John took Mary into his home and cared for her as his own mother.

John was a kindred spirit to our Lord. What a privilege that would be, but what pain John knew because of that special privilege! Kindred spirits can actually feel each other's joy. But they can also feel each other's pain, sorrow and grief.

When the tomb was found to be empty, the other disciples questioned what had happened to the body of Jesus, but not John. He knew a miracle was about to be revealed; He could feel it.

Jesus communicated so well with John that He chose him to write the great Revelation. It is a complicated book, full of complex symbolism which is very difficult for most Christians to interpret. But if it is hard to read and understand, can you imagine how hard it must have been to write? The descriptions John uses reveal to us that his spirit was knit together with the Spirit of the Lord.

Another pair of kindred spirits is David and Jonathan. Often it takes years to cultivate close friendship, but not when two spirits are as united as those of David and Jonathan were. The moment they met, there was a strong bond forged between them. This union of spirits went beyond social barriers. Jonathan was the son of the king of Israel. David was only a shepherd boy who had gained some notoriety by slaying the giant, Goliath. But 1 Samuel 20:17 tells us that David and Jonathan loved each other as they loved themselves. They made a covenant of love with one another so that their loyalty would be complete before the Lord.

Second Samuel 1:26 is part of a lament that David wrote for Jonathan after learning of the death of his friend in battle:

> "I grieve for you, Jonathan my brother;
>   you were very dear to me.
> Your love for me was wonderful,
>   more wonderful than that of women."

David did not find the intimate understanding that he and Jonathan shared, even with his own wife.

Many times it works out that we are kindred spirits with our mates — but not always. We develop a keen understanding of one another by living together, enjoying our leisure together, and worshipping together, but may not be kindred spirits. We most often compliment one another, but may never be able to interpret one another's deepest thoughts or desires without words.

When two spirits are united, no words are necessary between them. They share a silent knowledge and understanding.

Each of us needs a kindred spirit. We learn to understand ourselves better as we look into the heart of another. Proverbs 27:19 states:

> **As water reflects a face,**
> **so a man's heart reflects the man.**

There is a growth that takes place when we allow ourselves to be searched and known completely. There have been times when my kindred spirit has told me things about myself that I had never delved into enough to realize on my own. I trust my dear friend so much that I want to share with him my innermost thoughts.

When we are united in spirit, we share a deep love. We communicate spirit to spirit, without spoken words. We can be apart, but are always united one to the other. My love surrounds my kindred spirit always. Because our spirits are united, there is no need to hide, there is perfect trust.

As Shakespeare said, "Love reasons without reason."

8
Love Is Tough

"Love, it has been said, flows downward. The love of parents for their children has always been far more powerful than that of children for their parents; and who among the souls of men ever loved God with a thousandth part of the love which God has manifested to us?"

Hare

In our time in the ministry, my husband, Brian, and I have seen many troubled families. Family relations is an awkward area to work in. Children learn at such an early age how to manipulate their parents. This manipulation is especially evident in families in which the mother is left as a single parent. Not only is she expected to be the breadwinner of the family, but also a mother and homemaker as well. This heavy responsibility leaves her exhausted. Often it is easier to ignore or give in to the children than to discipline them. Such family situations are sad ones indeed, particularly for the children. By the time these young people are adolescents, they are often uncontrollable.

Parents of "problem children" may lament their mistakes, but regret and remorse will never change their teenager's current attitude and behavior. This type of situation requires what is often called "tough love."

One thing I have learned in my life and ministry is the fact that sentimentality and feelings of attachment are not the same as love. I have seen many parents who pamper their children, supplying them with their every need and desire. Many times such well-meaning, but sadly misinformed, parents produce children who become emotional cripples in their adult years.

The same thing happens to some of our people in institutions for the mentally or physically handicapped. They never learn how to make decisions for themselves because everything is always done for them by their well-intentioned, but overly protective, "caretakers."

True love is tough. When you truly love someone, that love gives you the divine ability to see the long-range picture. There is an old saying: "Give a man a fish, and he will eat today. Teach him how to fish, and he will eat for the rest of his life." This truth is especially applicable to child-rearing.

Insecure people have a hard time with the tough-love concept. They are so worried about being shown affection in return that they allow their children to rule (and often ruin) their home. I can still remember having coffee with a parent who was still supporting his "child" who was past thirty and without a job. All the "kid" did was lie around the house and mouth obscenities and threaten to kill his parents if they didn't give him his way. When a "child" throws temper tantrums at 30 years of age, it's past time to push him out of the nest into the real world! Remember, better late than never!

There are many parents who live in fear of their own children, but yet won't call the police because of a false sense of parental "love," or because they are too concerned with "what the neighbors will think."

A while back, I heard a radio sermon by Charles Stanley, pastor of the First Baptist Church of Atlanta. In his message, Rev. Stanley suggested, what I consider, a perfect solution for parents of troubled teens. He said that if your teenager becomes uncontrollable, wait until he has cooled down and then have a talk with him. Tell him that you are unable to handle him so you are turning him over to his heavenly Father. Make it plain that from now on it is God Who will be watching over and disciplining him.

According to Rev. Stanley, many a young person has come back to his parents after a few months, begging to be taken out of the Father's hands. Why? Because God loves His children enough to be tough with them. These young people straightened up their lives when their heavenly Father got tough with them.

Real love cares more about the other person's welfare than his affection.

Paul knew tough love. In the fifth chapter of 1 Corinthians he wrote to tell the church in Corinth how to deal with a troubled and unrepentant young man in their midst who was living in sin with his stepmother. Paul instructed the Corinthian church to expel the young man from their fellowship and to have nothing to do with him until he had turned from his sinful ways.

That's a hard pill to swallow, I know, especially when the young person to be expelled is your own child. It hurts to let go of our loved ones, to allow them to fall until they hit rock bottom and finally decide to get up and come back to us and to our Christian faith and values. But there comes a time when that action is the only solution left to us.

In the fifteenth chapter of Luke, Jesus tells us the story of the prodigal son. This young man was a real "con artist." He had no respect for authority and no desire for responsibility. He managed to wangle his share of the inheritance from his father, before it was due to come to him as the younger son — and certainly long before he was wise enough to know how to handle it wisely.

So, what did this clever but foolish young man do? He took his share of the family estate and moved far away where he could be free to "do his own thing." He got his own "pad," and began to engage in a life of dissipation and debauchery. He wasted his father's hard-earned assets on "wine, women, and song" — not to mention a group of fair-weather friends who bilked him out of every cent he had, then abandoned him when the money ran out. Finally, the young spendthrift found himself penniless, friendless, and homeless, wallowing in self-pity in a filthy pig sty.

What do you suppose would have happened if the father of that young man had sent him a little "care package" every now and then to "tide him over till payday"? As long as he had money coming in from "dear ole Dad," that young man would never have come to his senses. But his father was far too wise to prolong the lesson he knew his son so desperately needed to learn. He simply left the prodigal alone until he had "wised up" and changed his attitude. The son had left home as an irresponsible freeloader, but as a result of his father's tough love, he returned as a respectful, obedient son.

I once heard a story of a woman who loaned her daughter a little money to start out on when she moved away from home. From time to time she loaned her a small amount for groceries. Pretty soon the daughter needed car fare and rent money. After a while, the mother began to carry a great deal of guilt because, although she had the money to give her daughter, she realized that the girl was becoming an emotional cripple. Finally the mother made a firm decision to stop "loaning" money that was never repaid. Her daughter became angry and broke off all contact with her mother. For two years the woman heard nothing from her child. Then one day, the hurting mother received a telephone call. It was her beloved daughter who called to tell her mother how much she loved her and to thank her for her discipline. Because of the mother's actions, the daughter had learned to budget her money and had actually become a "budget consultant," helping others to exercise control over their finances.

Praise the Lord for tough love and tough parents! Many times this tough love hurts the one who exercises it as much as the one being disciplined. Often we parents suffer the most from our commitment to tough love. But, as in the case of this mother who prayed for her daughter for two long years before receiving the answer to her prayers, in the long run the results are well worth the effort!

First John is a book about love. Part of love is divine discipline. John tells us that if we claim to love God, but are living in sin or mistreating our brother, we are only fooling ourselves. In 1 John 5:2 he states that we show our love to others by carrying out God's commands for them. God sees the whole picture. He cares enough to expect His children to live up to their full potential. He allows us to skin our knees and fall flat on our faces occasionally so we will learn important lessons in life. He even allows us the privilege of shaking our fists in His face and venting our resentment against Him because He will not "let us off the hook."

Love is never satisfied until it brings out the best in the beloved, no matter how much it hurts.

In conclusion, I would like to share with you a little story which illustrates this point so well:

A man saw a butterfly fighting to free itself from a coccoon. As he watched the beautiful creature struggling so hard, his heart went out to it. He thought to himself, "I'll help this butterfly by freeing it from its struggle." He cut a hole in the coccoon and pulled the butterfly from its cage. But when the butterfly tried to fly, it suddenly fell to the ground. Its wings were not strong enough to support its weight. The man watched in sorrow as the poor creature flapped helplessly on the ground. In a few minutes it was dead.

That butterfly died because it had been "rescued" from the struggle which would have provided it the strength and stamina it needed to face life.

Love is tough. Love sees the necessity of the struggle.

9

Love Is a Motivator

"Divine love is a sacred flower, which in its early bud is happiness, and in its full bloom is heaven."

Hervey

When I became a licensed minister, I was assigned a mentor. All of us who are just starting out need the benefit of a trained, experienced teacher. The job of a mentor is that of a spiritual adviser. Our mentor is there to give us a shove when we need to move faster, or a word of caution when we need to slow down.

The Lord blessed me with a wonderful mentor. When I see Terry, my teacher, I am reminded of my Lord. When he speaks, I hear the voice of the Good Shepherd. His fatherly love motivates me to attempt great things, and consoles me when I fail to achieve them. On days when I feel as though I want to quit, in my mind's eye I see Terry's disappointed face, and I persevere.

It was 3:00 a.m. when Brian and I received the telephone call. One of the young people we dearly love had been in a terrible automobile accident. Before falling to pieces from anxiety and grief, his distraught mother told us there was absolutely no hope for Eric. He had suffered a serious brain stem injury. He showed no brain activity at all. The doctor had said it would be best to begin planning his funeral.

I remember seeing the tubes in Eric's arms and nose. The doctors had performed a tracheotomy on him, inserting a tube so he could breath through his throat because his sinus passages had been crushed. A part of his skull was missing. He lay in bed in a fetal position, perfectly motionless. It was such a shock. Just hours earlier he had been a beautiful, vigorous 18-year-old who thought he "had the world by the tail."

How do you communicate love to a motionless mass of bruised flesh with no brain activity? That is exactly what God called me to do four years ago. For hours on end I sat by Eric's bedside, talking to him, taking care of his needs and showing him the love of Christ. Little by little he began to show signs of recovery. It was very slow. A person doesn't just come out of a coma. He fights his way out. A twitch of an eye can have great significance, or none at all. But, through it all, hour after hour, my love surrounded Eric.

One day the doctor came in to check his "hopeless" patient.

"Doctor, Eric has been opening his eyes," I said optimistically. "I think he sees me."

Sadly, the doctor told me that it was just a reflex. I didn't believe him.

"Doctor," I insisted, "I truly believe Eric knows me."

Just then Eric raised his head up off the pillow, ever so slightly, and turned towards me. It was not a large movement; in fact, it was quite small. But right then the doctor and I both knew that Eric was coming back.

You see, love notices the small things.

That was in 1984. Today Eric is handicapped, but he knows the love of Jesus. That love motivated him to live. It also opened a new door for my husband and me to work in a ministry with the mentally and physically handicapped.

Like Eric, we all need mentors and spiritual parents who love us enough to motivate us.

When I think of love motivation I always think of the prophet Elisha. His story begins in 1 Kings 19. He was a student who learned much from his mentor. But it is important to note that a mentor always gains a great deal from his pupils.

At the beginning of 1 Kings 19 we see a very depressed prophet named Elijah. He feels alone and unappreciated, with no purpose in life. He wants to die. But that is not what God has in mind for him. The Lord tells Elijah that He wants him to train a student named Elisha.

Now you would think that God would have picked someone straight out of seminary to be the sole disciple of His most important living prophet. But God always does the unexpected. Elisha is nothing but a dirt farmer. He has no social standing or education, nothing to recommend him for such a high position of trust and responsibility — just a firm faith in God as his Father.

Now I would like for us to see the result of the God-ordained relationship between these two men. Elisha, the dirt farmer, turns out to be the most faithful friend Elijah the prophet ever had. As a matter of fact, Elisha follows his master around like a puppy. Any good student knows that his days with his teacher are numbered; therefore, it is important to glean eveything he can while he has the opportunity. In that respect, Elisha is a very good student.

In his heart Elijah knows that his time on earth is almost finished, and he wants to spare his disciple the pain of his leaving. (I believe Elijah also needed some time to himself to meditate and come to terms with his imminent departure for heaven.) But faithful Eisha will not leave his master's side, not even for a minute.

Finally, the prophet asks his faithful disciple, ..."**Tell me, what can I do for you before I am taken from you?**" (2 Kings 2:9a).

Elisha expresses what we all feel toward our beloved teachers in the Lord: ..."**Let me inherit a double portion of your spirit**"...(v. 9b).

That is love motivation. When we see our Lord in our teacher, we are motivated to fulfill dreams that have been left unfinished by the one we love so dearly. We want to soar to the heights of our love, and even higher, to the very heavens.

Love brings out better than our best.

In 2 Kings 2:11-14 we see a very touching scene as a chariot of fire suddenly appears and Elijah is taken away into heaven in a whirlwind. Elisha picks up the coat of his departed mentor. The coat is filled with the living memory of his beloved teacher and friend. Elisha takes the coat and strikes the water of the Jordan River with it. A path is miraculously created through the water so he can cross on dry land.

Love paves the way for us to go forward to do great things.

Love is the miracle that motivates us to shoulder heavy loads and dream impossible dreams. It impels us to climb the highest mountains, and then invites us to sit back and enjoy the view. It calls out to us:

> **Make haste, my beloved, and be thou like to a roe or to a young hart upon the mountains of spices.**
>
> **Song of Solomon 8:14 KJV**

Love is a motivator.

10

Love Is a Mother Giving Birth

"Love is an image of God, and not a lifeless image, but the living essence of the divine nature which beams full of all goodness."

Martin Luther

When I was 18 years old, I went to the doctor for a physical checkup. He looked me over and said, "Laurie, it may be hard for you to have children. In fact, it may be impossible." He cited a long clinical term ending in *syndrome* to describe my condition.

"Well, Doctor," I thought to myself, "how long do I have left?" But it was not a life-threatening disease. It was simply an internal female problem which did not affect my health, but which did decrease my chances of ever being able to bear children. I was relieved to hear that it was "nothing serious." After all, at 18 years of age, child-bearing was the least of my worries.

A few years after I was married, however, my attitude started to change. I grew to love other people's children and began to feel left out when the female group discussion inevitably turned to diapers and the price of school lunches. I experienced a hollow feeling inside on Mother's Day when all the other young married women were being honored by their families. I had to admit that receiving a brightly-wrapped present addressed to "Mommy" and signed with the dog's name was just not the same! Seriously, I felt a definite void in my life.

My mild depression lasted for some time before I came to fully realize why Brian and I were not blessed with children. With our ministry of working with mentally and physically handicapped people, we would not have the time to devote to a family of our own.

I can still remember what a hospital chaplain told me one time when I was fussing over a mentally handicapped young man I especially loved. "Laurie," he said, "you're a frustrated mother at heart." At the time I was angry at his remark, but it did motivate me to search myself and the Lord for an answer to it.

The Lord is so wonderful. He is such a comfort. He gave me a verse of scripture which put everything into proper perspective:

> ...it is written:
>
> "Be glad, O barren woman,
>   who bears no children;
> break forth and cry aloud,
>   you who have no labor pains;
> because more are the children of the
>   desolate woman
> than of her who has a husband."
>
> **Galatians 4:27**

The Lord told me in my spirit:

"Laurie, this verse was written about Sarah. She was barren for years. But her seed became a blessing for the nations. You will be the spiritual mother of many. Your seed will also bless many. You will experience the labor pains of a mother as you struggle to bring your children to My Son. You will cry the tears of a mother when they take their first step forward in their Christian faith. You will suffer sleepless nights as your spiritual adolescents face the peer pressure in their high schools, colleges, the work world, or other institutions of learning. You will suffer the loneliness of the empty nest when you must let go and allow these Christian children to mature into adult disciples. But I promise you, as soon as you finish nurturing one group of children, there will be more. Your work as a spiritual parent will never end."

What a blessing that message from the Lord was. Yes, I am a parent and I love my spiritual children. I also know that they love me. I too have spiritual parents whom I cherish. Now when Mother's Day comes, I hear the Lord say to my heart, "Happy Mother's Day," and I am proud.

Today we went to the hospital to visit my brother and sister-in-law. They have a beautiful new baby boy named Richard James Lechlitner. When I arrived, the mother and baby were preparing to go home. That tiny six-pound baby was so precious, yet so helpless. I have never seen Sandy, my sister-in-law, look so radiant. She was so beautiful, holding her baby. She looked tired, but so proud and happy.

Childbirth is quite painful, but new life comes forth. There is nothing that compares with the love of a mother for her child. She sees to her precious infant's every need.

Whether we are spiritual parents or have our own offspring, there is pain in the birth and growth of our children. When they are tiny babies, they need our constant care, but it is like a sharp knife in our hearts when we hear them say, "I can do it myself." As they grow and our prayers surround them, we have the greatest joy when we hear them say, "I am a Christian like my mom and dad." Then we know that our work is worthwhile and that our children are going down the road that leads to the same Heavenly Home toward which we are headed. There we will spend eternity with them and our Lord.

11

Love Is the Powerful Force That Created the Universe

"It is strange that men will talk of miracles, revelations, inspiration, and the like, as things past, while love remains."

Henry David Thoreau

In Genesis, Chapters 1 and 2, we see God creating the universe. Like any proud Father, He wants His children to live in Paradise. God plants the beautiful garden of Eden and places man in it, to tend and care for it. It is heaven on earth. There are lovely surroundings and full fellowship with the Almighty. But man fails. Through disobedience, he separates himself from God.

The Bible sets forth God's plan to draw man back into fellowship with Him. How God must grieve over mankind's willful disobedience. But God never meant for us human beings to be puppets. He gave us a will of our own and the freedom to exercise that will.

Despite our fallen state, God still provides us with all things for our enjoyment. (1 Tim. 6:17.) The purple dawn and the radiant sunset are tokens of His love. Even the rain that falls and makes the grass green and our crops grow is a sign of God's never-ending love and continual provision for His beloved creation.

A few years ago, I went to the Atlantic Ocean. I love the sea. As I stood there on the shore, I was filled with wonder and awe at the huge, endless expanse which lay before me. The seagulls called noisily to one another and the waves were strong and majestic as they thundered in at high tide. I can still remember the salty taste I would get in my mouth as the sprays of water hit the air. Walking on the beach in the warm sunshine was pleasant, but I also liked to amble along the seashore when the skies were grey and overcast.

You see, the ocean has a personality that is affected by the weather. When the sun is shining and the sky is clear, the sea is gay and carefree. But on a windy, overcast day, it becomes loud and forceful. It thunders out its praise to God in all seriousness.

When I saw the ocean for the first time, it reminded me of God's majesty, of His great splendor and power. Proverbs 8:29 came to my mind:

> ...he gave the sea its boundary
> so the waters would not overstep his
> command....

God is awesome in power. So is love. In fact, love *is* power. There is energy and authority in love. God's love and power are too wonderful for man to fully comprehend. We see this love and power evidenced in the exodus of God's people from Egypt. It was God's powerful love which parted the Red Sea so the children of Israel could walk through it on dry ground.

In the nineteenth chapter of the book of Exodus, we see another demonstration of the power of God's love. God tells Moses to consecrate the Israelites because His presence is going to come down on Mount Sinai. As the people stand to meet their Creator, the whole mountain trembles and is engulfed with fire and smoke. When God speaks, the people shake in fright and beg for a mediator, someone to spare them from the shock of the awesome presence of the Almighty.

I have always had a special place in my heart for Moses. He spoke to God as a man to his friend.

In Exodus 33:18-23 Moses actually has the courage to ask God if he can see Him in all His glory. Moses really doesn't know what he is asking. God is so kind. He loves Moses so much. But He reminds him, ..."...**you cannot see my face, for no one may see me and live**" (v. 20). So God puts Moses in the cleft of a rock while His glory passes by. Moses sees the back of God, but not His face.

I have always wondered why mankind cannot gaze directly into the face of God. But I think it must be because of the perfect love that is there. The power of God's pure love would overcome any mortal man.

I, like Moses, want to see God in all His glory. I want to gaze upon His face.

My husband and I live in a wooded area and I thoroughly enjoy it. There is such an active array of wildlife and nature to observe in my own yard. I love to get up early in the morning when it is still hazy. The dew is on the grass and the birds are chirping and digging for their breakfast.

One particular day this past summer, I was sitting outside on my favorite swing. It's a porch swing, but we have it suspended between two trees. The scene before me was so calm and peaceful, and I was so aware of the presence of the Lord, I was moved to ask God if I could see His glory. He answered me in a rather unpredictable way. At His inspiration, I took pen in hand and, as I wrote, I experienced God's glory. This is a page from my journal, dated August 5, 1987:

"Lord,

"Teach me to seek Your face. Let me be present in Your glory. Let me follow You to the mysteries of the ages. I want to follow You in the pathway of the wind of Your Spirit. I want to know Your mind and feel Your heart. I want to laugh and cry with You.

"I want to know the solitude of Your guidance, as well as the community of Your people.

"I want to run the 'good race' with Paul. I want to watch with Moses as the Red Sea parts. I want to be carried in the flaming chariot of a whirlwind like Elijah. I want to find joy in being crucified with Christ.

"I want to see Your mark of divine blessing on the poverty-stricken, the crippled, the prisoners, the blind, and those with mental and physical disabilities.

"I want to bear others' burdens and make the oppressed smile.

"I want to see my sinful condition, but rejoice in the righteousness I have in Christ.

"I want to live and die in You. Only then can I see Your face in its completeness."

The Lord has blessed me and allowed me to see His glory pass by, but not to see His face in its completeness.

God's love created the heavens and the earth. Each blade of grass, each flower and tree bears God's insignia. Each has a personality all its own. No two roses are completely alike, but they are completely beautiful.

God's power is awesome.

One day as I was out in my yard, the Lord spoke to me in my spirit:

"Look at that big oak tree. It reaches to the sky. It has weathered rain and snow and strong winds. But one bolt of lightning from My hand could send it crashing to the ground."

That's power!

God's love is the powerful force that created the universe.

12
Love Is the Gift of God — Himself!

"Love is the greatest thing that God can give us for Himself is love; and it is the greatest thing we can give to God, for it will also give ourselves, and carry with it all that is ours. The apostle calls it the bond of perfection; it is the old, the new, and the great commandment, and all the commandments, for it is the fulfilling of the law. It does the work of all the other graces without any instrument but its own immediate virtue."

Jeremy Taylor

Then God said, "Let us make man in our image...."

Genesis 1:26

God loves mankind. He has loved us since Creation. I pity the people who see God as some faraway deity Who created the world and put man in charge of it so He would be freed to concern Himself with other, more pressing, matters.

So many times I hear people say, "Why should God concern Himself with my problems?" I believe God is deeply hurt by this kind of attitude.

Jesus Christ came to the earth to show us the true nature of God. Greater love has no man than to lay down his life for his friends. (John 15:13.) This is what Jesus did for us. He was the tangible representative of God's love. No wonder few recognized Him. They saw

71

their Creator as a judgmental God of wrath. But Jesus showed us that He is a gentle, loving Father.

In Luke 11, when the disciples ask Jesus to teach them how to pray, He begins His model prayer by addressing God as "Our Father." (Luke 11:2 KJV.) When we learn to see God as a loving Father, our blurred vision will start to clear and we will come to know Him as He really is.

A friend of mine once rebuked me when I told her, "I don't want to hurt God, my Father; I don't want to make Him cry."

"I don't believe God can be hurt," she replied sharply, "and I certainly don't believe He cries."

I strongly disagree with my friend. I find in scripture that God laughs and He cries. Psalm 2:4 tells us that God laughs at the rulers of the earth who plot against His Anointed One.

God sees the "big picture," the ultimate end of everything. Often, I believe, He laughs with us when we get ourselves into humorous situations. I remember quite well one such situation in my own life.

The first time I preached at my home church, I became very nervous. I had preached in other churches, but it is always different when you get up to speak to your own people. These folks are my church family and I love them dearly. They know me so well.

I began my sermon just great. But when I get nervous, my mouth dries out. After I had been talking for about five minutes, my mouth had dried completely shut. I could only open it a crack, just enough to utter strange noises. I kept motioning to my husband to get me a drink of water. It took him about five minutes to find a glass in the kitchen downstairs. All the time I was making wild gestures and unintelligible sounds, trying to explain to the congregation what was going on.

By the time I had finally got my drink and could talk again, half of the congregation was stricken with laughter and the other half was valiantly trying to conceal their amusement. I got through the sermon, but was crushed. I felt totally humiliated and thought that my world had come to an end. Furthermore, I made up my mind right then that never again did I want to face the people in my home church! I went home and wept bitterly, vowing that I was going to move far away where no one had even heard of me.

Just then I felt the presence of the Lord. In my spirit I could sense His wonderful peace and love. I also felt His gentle laughter. My world was no longer at an end. The Father and I laughed and laughed together. I still laugh when I recall that incident. And I know my Father is proud of me — even when my lips stick together.

God and I not only laugh together, we also cry together. In Jeremiah 14:17 we read where God cries for His people, Israel. He instructs His prophet:

> **"Speak this word to them:**
> **" 'Let my eyes overflow with tears**
> **night and day without ceasing;**
> **for my virgin daughter — my people —**
> **has suffered a grievous wound,**
> **a crushing blow.' "**

One Wednesday evening I came home exhausted. I had taught two Bible studies that day and had just received the distressing news that one of our youth had been admitted to the hospital with a serious illness. A few of my flock were suffering with problems, spiritually and emotionally. When I finally got home, I just sat down and wept. I was not crying for myself, but for my dear people.

"Dear Lord," I said, "how can I help my people? Their problems are so great."

In my spirit I knew that the Lord understood. I knew that He too had compassion because I could feel His tears and His fatherly embrace.

God loves us. He is a personal God. He feels what we feel. He laughs and cries with us. Since the beginning of Creation, He has sought communion with us. In the garden of Eden, He cried out to Adam, . . ."**Where are you?**" (Gen. 3:9).

Today He still reaches out His hand of love to us. When we are too busy to respond, He is lonely. He knows the thorns of love and the pain of rejection, as well as the joy of love, new birth, and growth. When the arms of our spirits reach out to Him, we will feel the loving embace of our heavenly Father.

God not only knows love, He *is* love.

About the Author

Laurie Lechlitner is in her second year as a licensed minister in the Church of the Brethren. She and her husband, Brian, specialize in ministering to those in institutions such as hospitals, prisons and facilities for the mentally and physically handicapped. They have been involved in this ministry for eight years.

Writing is one of Laurie's hobbies. Each week she prepares a newsletter for members of her fellowship, Baugo Church of the Brethren. She also enjoys Bible teaching and preaching. A lover of the great outdoors, Laurie has learned many things about the Creator by observing His creatures.

Laurie welcomes correspondence from her readers. Comments, questions and prayer/counsel requests should be addressed to:

Laurie Lechlitner
P. O. Box 852
Wakarusa, Indiana 46573

NOTES

NOTES

NOTES